This is Me: Memories and Musings of a Thirtysomething

Ashley Sanders

BookLeaf Publishing

India | USA | UK

Presentation by *BookLeaf Publishing*

Web: www.bookleafpub.com

E-mail: info@bookleafpub.com

ISBN: 9789363314450

First edition 2024

For all of the wallflowers,

you deserve to be seen and heard.

ACKNOWLEDGEMENT

First of all, I would like to thank Sam, whose lyrics and charm sparked my urge to write for the first time in over 12 years. He was my inspiration, and for that, I will be forever grateful.

To my dear friends Shameika, Ashlen, Nicole and Amy Loerke (rhymes with turkey) who listened to anything and everything I was going through without judgment. They were the first to read any of my poems and provided me with honest feedback and loads of encouragement. Without Amy, I would not have learned of the poetry challenge that led to this book being published.

To my wonderful coworker, Roberta, whose kind words about my writing gave me the confidence to feel like a real writer and was the final shove I needed to decide to actually pursue publishing.

Next, I have to thank my cousin, Candice. She has shown unwavering support and love for anything I wish to do in life, and writing has been no different. She absolutely hates to read, but still took the time to read my poems and lend an opinion. Upon hearing of the poetry challenge, she insisted I take part and wouldn't accept "no" for an answer. Thank you for believing in me and all the things.

Lastly, I wish I could thank everyone by name who has encouraged me along this journey, but that would take a whole book in itself. I've received nothing but support from the rest of my family, my closest friends, my church family, my amazing coworkers, and my fellow Dolls. I am truly blessed with the best people.

PREFACE

Writing was something I enjoyed immensely in high school - so much so, I took Creative Writing no less than 3 times. Through rewrites and resubmissions, I came so close (9.9) but never achieved the coveted, perfect score of 10. Eventually, life got busy and writing became a hobby of the past by the time I graduated college in 2012.

Some of the memories I've written for this book have been stored for so long in the recesses of my brain - almost always at surface level and ready for recall at a moment's notice. The thoughts of wanting to get my memories and feelings down on paper have been at the back of my mind throughout my entire adult life. Recent self-discoveries have catapulted my hunger for writing back to the forefront. Once lost dreams are making their way to the surface and have reignited those passions within me that I thought would never return. I've grown tired of thinking about one day writing a poetry book and decided to just go for it.

These writings are autobiographical - they are traumas and losses I've lived through, joyous moments I want to re-experience, and the dreams and hopes I hold for my future.

It is my hope that sharing my stories will help others to know that while their experiences are their own, we can all relate to one another in some way. It is also my hope that if anyone is experiencing any trauma or grief, that they know they are not alone. We were not put on this beautiful planet to do life alone, but in circles - share your stories and let us heal together.

Content Warning: Allusions to and mentions of death/grief, domestic violence, sexual assault of a child, and drug addiction.

Dad

How I would have loved to have known you.
All I have are the stories passed down to me
from those who knew you best,
They make me ache for what could have been.

A sandy-haired boy with blue eyes and thick
glasses,
Large build and the Sanders' nose,
you would often bring home animals that needed
saving;
all traits passed on to me and John.

I'll randomly ask and mom will regale me with
the tale of the day I was born;
they handed me to you and you looked up,
crying -
"We have a little girl!"
You chose the name Ashley, mom chose the
name Daile.

She said I was a daddy's girl,
that I was your whole world.
You'd already have me out of my carseat and
into your arms before mom could even close her
car door.

We had a special bond only a daddy and his
daughter could share.

You taught me to use your first CD player
and I'd blast Queen in the middle of the night.
You cultivated a love for music in me
I can only imagine the concerts you would have
taken me to see.

I often wonder how much different life would be
if you had been around to help me grow.
I think about your unfulfilled dreams of having a
large family;
I wonder how many siblings I'd have,
if I'd be married and have kids of my own by
now.

Your death would go on to have devastating
consequences for years.
A careless act by your desperate brother
would leave my mom without a husband
And me and John without a father.

In a rush to recover something someone took
He drunkenly drove you into a tree
And stole you away from all of us
When I was only three.

Core Memory

Euphoric with wind rushing through my golden
hair
racing from opposite ends of the block to see
who'd win,
only to collide on the front lawn among a sea of
bicycles;
a mountain forever present in the yard
of our cherry-picked neighborhood mother.

My provisional dwelling in the summer months,
I rarely left; felt more like home than home.
But I missed my mom.
My brother stayed behind at our amiable refuge;
I should have stayed, too.

Alone on the lawn, a hapless descent upon the
jumble of twisted metal at my feet.
Perfect angle of gear striking skin;
a rugged gash sullied my sun-kissed knee.
Instant stream of warmth and viscousness
flowed.
I should have stayed then, too.

Two blocks I limped leaning against a purple
crutch on wheels.

Wary onlookers peep through curtains drawn,
but no one stops to help the little girl with the
shredded visage.
Such a painfully long hobble to get home to the
only person who can kiss it and make it better;
I need my mommy, but she is not there.

Suddenly a nurse at the tender age of nine,
wistfully and gently mucking away the mess of
red congealed down my leg.
Damp cloth acting as my bandage.
A glass of water and a carefully propped leg
high on the sofa that is my new stronghold.
My leg is too painful and stiff to move, so the
remote becomes my savior;
usually absent of any power source,
it bolsters my company in the form of The
NeverEnding Story III on loop.

Hours pass by; a constant ache in my knee and
my chest.
At 3AM she finally appears long enough to refill
my glass of water,
Not even staying to hear about my fall, in a
perpetual search for her next high
while I lay wondering when she will leave her
recreation for me as I left mine for her.

White Sugar

For as long as I can remember, you've been a
chaser
searching for minuscule specks of white amid
maroon carpet fibers
On a constant quest after that ephemeral 5
minute rush each hit brings.
It gives so little in comparison to what it takes
away.

Commandeered years and unformed memories
haunt my psyche.
What life could have been - could STILL be, if
you were not devoted to this invisible ball and
chain.
It's hard to imagine a life in which synthetic
poisons hadn't stolen you away from us,
it's all we've ever known.

Friendships ended by neighboring parents
watching our furniture being shoved out onto the
front lawn.
Rarely having a home phone line and frequently
having our utilities shut off due to non-payment.
Asking to be in soccer and gymnastics and being
told "no" because we could not afford it.

There were days we didn't even eat.

Fast forward to the current - I ask you all the
time if you want to work on getting clean, you
don't.
You choose this pestilence in lieu of what could
be a beautiful life.
There is still time - I don't know how much - to
make lasting memories; ones we can look back
on fondly
But rather than hold onto us, you hold onto your
crack pipe.

Fears of Atlas

Condemned to carry the weight of your
addiction, my shoulders dare to buckle,
except I didn't revolt against the gods, so why
am I the one being punished?
This isn't a burden I was meant to carry, is it?

You've struggled with this affliction since I was
a little kid, now into my 30s.
Living in the clutch of this tyrannical, illicit
deity for far too long
a foreboding monument always casting shade
over my quiet town.

The forcible size threatens to squash me
at times, I've wanted to let it send me on an
unreturnable journey
I might have let it if it had not been for the
fortitude bestowed upon me by my Redeemer.

I don't feel particularly strong, but I must be to
have made it this far.
I've been to hell and back.
you keep sending me there and I always find my
way to the start
one day, I fear I'll get lost on the return voyage

my mind's tendencies, so akin to yours, are
buried just beneath the surface;
one slip and it's all over.

I've worked too diligently to get where I am
today
to fall victim to my genetic predispositions.
I learned from your mistakes; I'll be damned if
I'm to repeat them.

But the intrusive fears remain, a constant
reminder of the fall of Adam.
Will I collapse under the weight? Fold to the
same proclivities that prompt unwanted habits?
I'm now the same age you were when you lost
the battle and your plight began.

Luisa

Like you, Luisa, I bear a familial weight on my
shoulders
Ultimately, the burden of decision-making often
lies with me alone
Impossible at times, it seems; but
Strength drawn from a life lived hard has made
me surprisingly
Adept to take on life's challenges.

The Outcast

Today I stand alone in the changing room at the
Y.
I've isolated myself out of shame and none of
you know the reason.
Perhaps you think I'm odd, or that I'm maybe
too shy.
Or maybe you think I don't know how to swim.

The truth is, I was so excited for today.
I wore three swimsuits to bed because I couldn't
decide which to wear.
My best friend is turning 11!
I don't have many friends, but she does; I'm
hoping we become friends, too.

Only, how can we be friends if I keep hiding
away?
I attempt to act normal and get in the pool with
all of you,
But it just hurts too much;
every wade sends ripples of stinging pain
through my broken body.

With every ounce of dignity I have left,

I slowly make my way to the opposite end of the
pool and climb out.
I walk sheepishly so you don't see me leaving,
I don't want to ruin Heather's birthday.

I give no indication that last night was the
scariest night of my life.
None of you know that while you had chosen
which swimsuit to wear,
Mine was being ripped off of my body and
tossed in the corner,
Thrown away as casually as my innocence.

No one talked to me today.
My self-seclusion was a deterrent that would go
on to last for years.
I just wanted friends. Needed a friend.
But today I stand alone.

Tread Marks

There are these scars, like tread marks on my heart
That remain with me every single day.
I can still hear his teeth grinding in my head so loud it can break any silence;
Shivers prickle down my neck when I think back to being awoken by that cruel sound.
The fear I experienced while being marched to that beige shed, a place of nightmares.
Playboy pin-up pictures on the walls stared at me
As they were forced to watch something they did not wish to see.
The radio played hard rock to stifle my pleading and my sobs;
a scratchy, yellow couch stained with the remnants of my innocence.

I still drive by my childhood house to glance at the shed that still stands,
a reminder of the torment that lingers long after the pain has been inflicted,
and the unabashed surety that you did not break me.

The Bear

The bear wouldn't rip my bathing suit off and
throw it in the corner.
The bear wouldn't wipe up my vomit with my
baby blanket.
The bear wouldn't tell me to be quiet so I
wouldn't wake anyone up.
The bear wouldn't lie and say they'd never hurt
me again.
The bear wouldn't threaten to kill my friends
and family if I told anyone.
The bear wouldn't tell his buddies that a 10 year
old was in love with him.
The bear wouldn't rape me before school and
then send me to wait for the bus.

Monsters are Real

The monster snapped it jaws,
saliva dripping from pointed teeth.
hunger grumbling in his belly, lurking
down the red carpeted hall toward her door,
heat projected from huffing nostrils
as he sniffed in search of his next meal.
head ducked to enter through the door frame
as the princess lay hiding under the covers in
these four pink walls.
rushing into her room, her daddy shielded her
with his body;
like magic, the monster disappeared.

No matter how many times her daddy chased
away the monster in her dreams,
he could never save her from the waking
nightmare;
He could only look down from heaven
as a real life monster
breached the safety of those same pink walls
also in search of his next meal
to satisfy a different type of hunger.
sliding his calloused hands where they ought not
be,
she wiggled and pretended to sleep

as he betrayed the princess he was chosen to protect.

Relinquished Friendship

I spend most of my time wondering why.
Concentration has become so futile
In the two weeks since you said your goodbye.
Who knew one could feel something so brutal.
So many feelings pour out of my eyes,
They dry up, failing to give what they must,
Leaving me with a need undone, your prize.
Woe you gave, was your dissolution just?
Me not knowing is an understatement
To this denouement, what was the purpose?
Justification for this, you haven't,
Ardently you filled yourself with bogus.
Spotting only false, when fact you foraged,
Something I unknowingly encouraged.

Turnkey

"You would be so pretty if you were skinny"
they told me. And I told myself.
"You are so chill and easy to talk to"
just not that easy to kiss, right?

Neglectful parenting and repressed childhood
traumas
led me down a path of destructive self-harm in
the form of binge eating.
I ate when I was sad, when I was angry, when I
was bored.
I ate when I was already full.

I spent my teen years wondering if anyone could
love the fat girl
hiding behind hoodies and books.
College was the same - any qualities I actually
felt might be worthy
always overlooked because I was heavy.

I thought getting physically healthy would give
me a confidence boost;
help me be more mentally sound.
It was just a lie I told myself.

How am I becoming more confident but even
more insecure at the same time?

Sure I feel great now, but I look at myself in the
mirror
and all I see are white stretch marks plaguing my
smaller frame due to overindulgence.
I put on a cute outfit, only to stare at the
collection of loose skin around my lower
abdomen.
my arms - wings poised to fly me back into a
safer space of longer sleeves.

I'm so damn tired of hiding.
Society is shifting to a beautiful place where all
bodies are being praised
but I'm still trapped in the confines of my own
mind
my temple is in ruins, and not the kind admired
for its former wonder.

I want to be loved - for ALL of me.
but I've secured and padlocked all of my doors
too afraid to try because of all my past fears of
future rejections
and I'm the only one holding the key.

See Me

Will you see me the way others see me?

Will you notice that I treat those around me with
kindness?
Or that I feel others' pain so deeply, I weep with
them?
That I am both shy and extroverted at the same
time?
That I can strike up a conversation with anyone,
anywhere?
Will you see the blue of my eyes that I inherited
from my dad?

Or will you see me the way I see myself?

Will you pick up on any of the emotional
damages dealt by life?
Will your eyes focus on the parts of me I stare at
in the mirror?
The extra skin that remains after weight loss?
The lashes so blonde it looks as if I have none?
The thinning hair that I inherited from my mom?

I want so hard to see myself the way others see
me.
Which version of me will you see?

Glue

When first applied, it is strong.
Bonds forged in cement with no signs of
budging.
Over time, its composition changes, not unlike
other materials.
Eventually, it breaks down and loses its
cohesiveness.

Our family was once held carefully together by
your adherence.
Sickness stripped you away leaving behind a
tacky residue.
We are doing our best to hold together what's
left,
But paper clips and frayed fibers aren't sturdy
enough.

The glue has turned yellow and retains none of
its original adhesiveness.
The last pieces of you in my possession are
being held together by double-sided tape
In the scrapbook of my memory
Which, over time, will, too, deteriorate.

In the Waiting

I'm exhausted.
Stuck
between what my head and heart are persuading
me to do,
Each pulling me in opposite directions.
Uncertainty
in every choice I've ever made, or will make
from here on out.

It's like the anxiety you experience just before a
roller coaster,
Only
you know this won't be fun once you get on.
I just want it to be over already
but I can't quite seem to step into the buggy.

I just stand there, staring at what I've decided is
the inevitable
avoiding it at all costs
while those around me aren't anxious, but
excited
they ask me what I'm waiting for, and
tell me the best part begins just beyond the hill.

Molting

One by one, my feathers disappeared;
Dreams that simply floated away with the wind.
I watched each one being swept away in an
updraft,
I gave up reaching out to try and catch them.
One day I looked down to realize
the only feathers that remained were broken.
What is it to live if there are no more dreams?

But in order for new feathers to grow,
the old ones must be lost.
Plucking the rest of my damaged plumage,
I'm finally permitting new dreams to grow in
their place.
and what beautiful feathers they are, indeed.

Still, Small Moments

It's in the still, small moments that I learn the
most about myself
in the quiet
when it is just me and my thoughts.
They consume me sometimes,
taking hold of a particular anxiety and drawing
from its power over me
until I shrink back to the refuge of my bedspread
and
the comforting smell of my faithful pillow.
Ill will plagues my every thought,
"You can't," "you won't," "what'll you do?"
I'll breathe and trust that God has a plan for me.

Chasing a Daydream

I want the still, calm, quiet of the early morning.
Sitting in the crisp, dewy air in this isolated
place.
Trees bring this space to life.
A gentle breeze rustling the leaves as flecks of
sun escape the canopy and dance across the
pages of my book.
The aroma of freshly brewed coffee wafting
from the mug I hold with both hands, the
warmth a stark contrast to the chill in the air.
Our shoulders touch as we sit side by side on
your porch and stare out at the woodsy
landscape before us.
You tuck a tuft of hair behind my ear and I rest
my head upon your shoulder.
These subtle affections make my heart blush; it
gushes with adoration knowing it's tended well.
You could keep me here forever and I would be
content.

Tennessee

Sunlight peeks through tall windows and casts a
glow on the slanted ceilings.
I hear the ticking of the many clocks carefully
placed in this house that make it a home.
The luscious green of the Dwarf Mountain Pines
are picturesque,
a heavenly backdrop that encourages these
words to flow.
The mountains are my place of comfort and ease
and I never want to leave.

Trapped

I feel like a moth stuck between the window and
the screen,
desperately attempting to break through the
vinyl-coated mesh to get to my freedom and the
fresh air I can smell through the teensy holes.
On the other side there is a clear view to the life
I was in such a hurry to leave behind,
protected by the thick fiberglass that serves as a
sturdy wall.
Try as I might, my fragile body cannot penetrate
either barrier
and I'm left here in my purgatory to ponder the
aftermath of my choices.

The Catalyst

The dreams were always there,
a meager pile of kindling, carefully stacked over time;
it became doused when I started to feel stuck.
I spent years knowing there was something more for me out there.
But I settled into what I thought was comfort;
Not knowing how to change my situation,
not really trying.
It wasn't comfort, it was a fear;
a fear of change and a fear for the unknown.
I stopped adding to the pile -
no more dreams, no growth, no more goals for myself.

Then one day, I discovered a lumberjack;
an awkward, charming, hilarious lumberjack.
I felt this immediate sadness for myself
And this overwhelming nostalgia for lost hopes.
A lot of the traits I saw in the lumberjack
were the things I knew I was missing out on the opportunity of finding
because I was too scared to go after them.
If I was denying myself the possibility of true happiness in a partner,

what else was I depriving myself of?
The answer is everything.

It first took realizing that I had allowed myself
to become stagnant.
For the first time in my adult life,
I settled into a career with no room for
advancement.
Previously, my ambition was to climb as far as I
could go
but I hit a rung on the ladder that was a little
more spacious than the rest
and I lingered there for too long -
each step that followed seemed more tedious
than the last,
and I gave up.

Then the lumberjack turned my whole world
upside down.
You see, he was my catalyst;
the spark I needed to reignite the aspirations I
once held.

The last five months have been a whirlwind of
change,
and a hurricane of emotions.
I started to envision what my life could be
if I found the person truly meant for me,

rather than merely existing with someone out of
ease;
it brought to an end a relationship that fizzled
out many moons ago.
I began writing again, something I had not done
in years,
and I will be a published poet before the summer
is over.
An opportunity for a new career path with
endless possibilities has been presented to me -
all because I took a step outside of my comfort
zone,
and decided the risk was finally worth the
reward.

The lumberjack's spark was all I needed to
ignite the kindling I had carefully collected over
the years;
gradually, I started adding new sticks, and these
desires
fueled the tiny flames that have since grown into
a full-fledged conflagration,
threatening to destroy the life I'm poised to
leave behind,
and I will let it burn.

An Ode to Autumn

Browns, reds, oranges and yellows in all their
glory,
that crispness in the air so permeable you can
smell it
freshness, newness
twinge of cold raises goosebumps
ragweed clings to my nose with a vice grip
light breeze lends to clear thoughts
and hope for novel beginnings
football games that bring me closer to my uncle
hot soups and even hotter cider keep my hands
and belly warm on nippy autumn nights
bonfires bring us together for s'mores, good
music and great company.